AF595797
N
W
E
S
QLD
QUEENSLAND
SA
SOUTH
AUSTRALIA
NSW
NEW SOUTH WALES
ACT
AUSTRALIAN
CAPITAL
TERRITORY
VIC
VICTORIA
TAS
TASMANIA

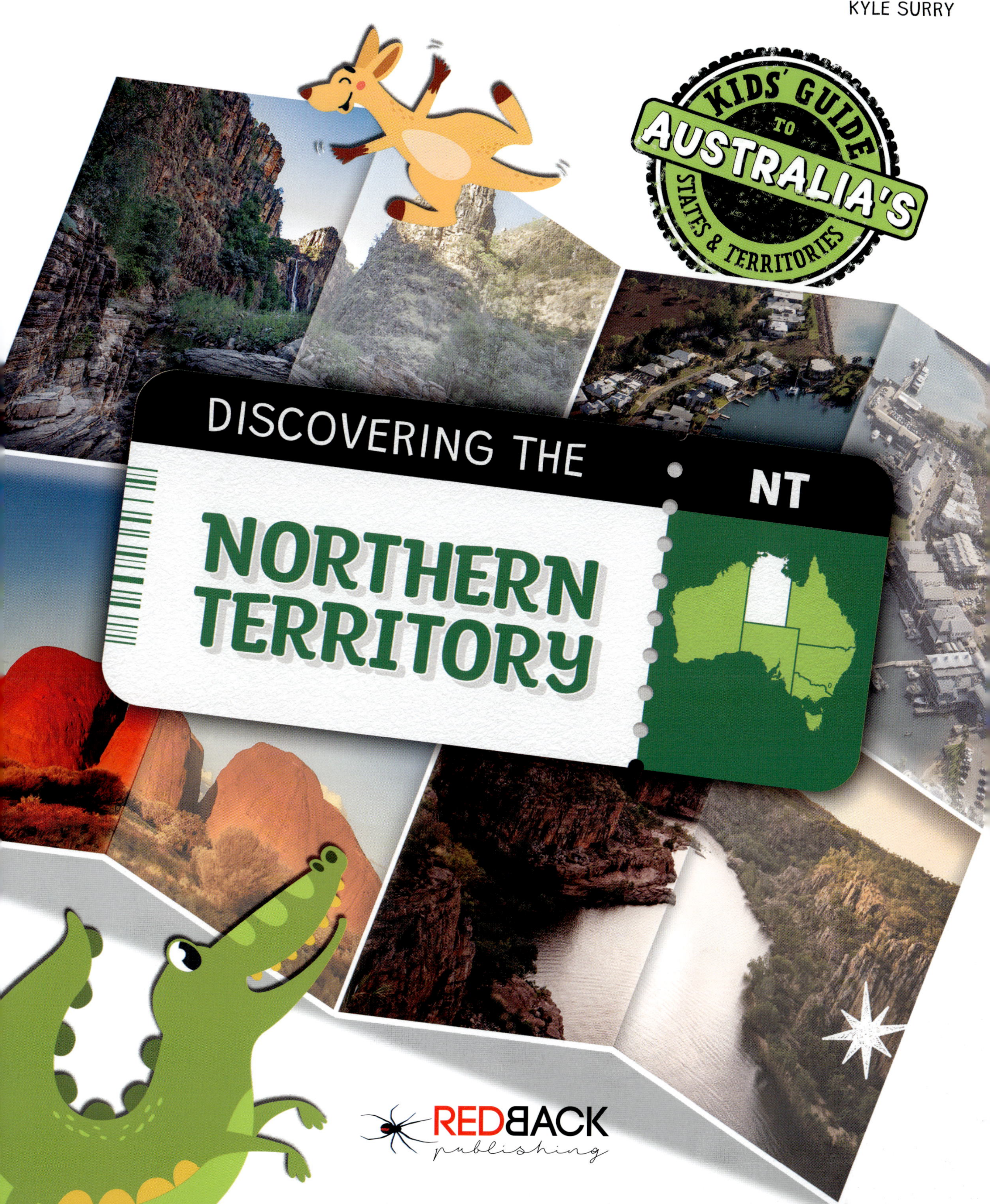
KYLE SURRY
KIDS' GUIDE TO AUSTRALIA'S STATES & TERRITORIES
DISCOVERING THE
NT
NORTHERN TERRITORY
REDBACK publishing

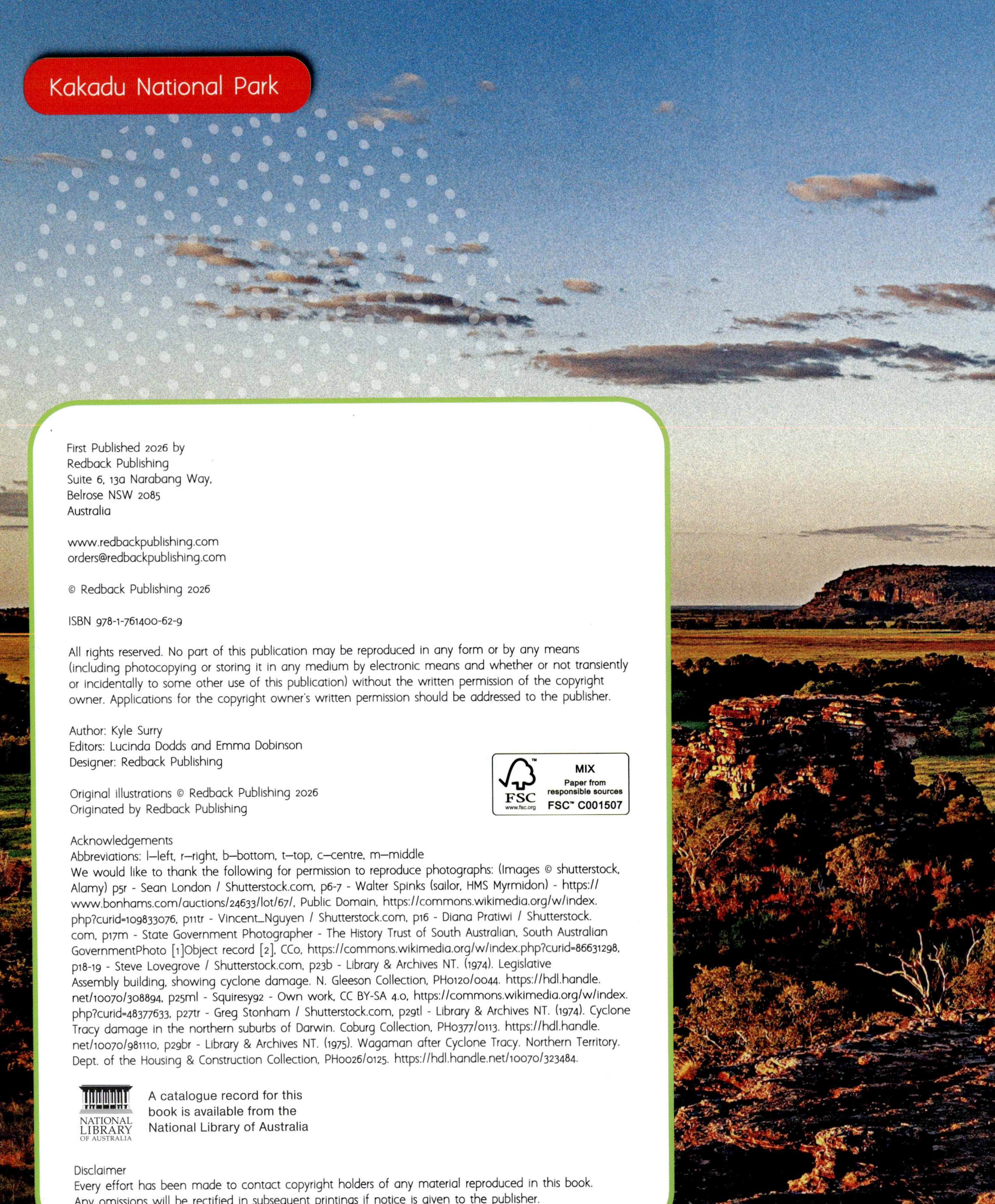

First Published 2026 by
Redback Publishing
Suite 6, 13a Narabang Way,
Belrose NSW 2085
Australia

www.redbackpublishing.com
orders@redbackpublishing.com

ISBN 978-1-761400-62-9

Author: Kyle Surry
Editors: Lucinda Dodds and Emma Dobinson
Designer: Redback Publishing

Original illustrations © Redback Publishing 2026
Originated by Redback Publishing

MIX
Paper from responsible sources
FSC www.fsc.org FSC™ C001507

Acknowledgements
Abbreviations: l—left, r—right, b—bottom, t—top, c—centre, m—middle
We would like to thank the following for permission to reproduce photographs: (Images © shutterstock, Alamy) p5r - Sean London / Shutterstock.com, p6-7 - Walter Spinks (sailor, HMS Myrmidon) - https://www.bonhams.com/auctions/24633/lot/67/, Public Domain, https://commons.wikimedia.org/w/index.php?curid=109833076, p11tr - Vincent_Nguyen / Shutterstock.com, p16 - Diana Pratiwi / Shutterstock.com, p17m - State Government Photographer - The History Trust of South Australian, South Australian GovernmentPhoto [1]Object record [2], CC0, https://commons.wikimedia.org/w/index.php?curid=86631298, p18-19 - Steve Lovegrove / Shutterstock.com, p23b - Library & Archives NT. (1974). Legislative Assembly building, showing cyclone damage. N. Gleeson Collection, PH0120/0044. https://hdl.handle.net/10070/308894, p25ml - Squiresy92 - Own work, CC BY-SA 4.0, https://commons.wikimedia.org/w/index.php?curid=48377633, p27tr - Greg Stonham / Shutterstock.com, p29tl - Library & Archives NT. (1974). Cyclone Tracy damage in the northern suburbs of Darwin. Coburg Collection, PH0377/0113. https://hdl.handle.net/10070/981110, p29br - Library & Archives NT. (1975). Wagaman after Cyclone Tracy. Northern Territory. Dept. of the Housing & Construction Collection, PH0026/0125. https://hdl.handle.net/10070/323484.

NATIONAL LIBRARY OF AUSTRALIA
A catalogue record for this book is available from the National Library of Australia

CONTENTS

A LONG TIME AGO

Arnhem Land

Indigenous Australians were living in Arnhem Land, in the north of the Northern Territory, over 65,000 years ago. The oldest stone tools ever found in Australia were in Arnhem Land.

Dot Painting

The dot style of painting has been used by Indigenous Australians for thousands of years.

Land Rights

Traditional land rights for about half of the Northern Territory have been returned to local Indigenous peoples.

SETTLERS AND COLONISERS

The Northern Territory was included in the land claimed by Britain in 1788, when the first British settlers arrived in Sydney. In 1863, the Northern Territory became a part of South Australia. In 1869, after five attempts at settlement failed, Britain finally created the town of Palmerston. This later became the city of Darwin.

1911

The new Australian Government took control of the Northern Territory.

1978

The Northern Territory gained its own government, while still being a territory of the Commonwealth of Australia.

Port Darwin

1998

people in the Northern Territory voted NO to becoming a state of Australia. They wanted to remain as a territory instead.

WHERE IS THE NORTHERN TERRITORY?

The Northern Territory is the largest territory of Australia. Its shortened name is written as NT. Darwin on the northern coast is the capital city.

Some people just call the NT 'the Territory'. There are other territories in Australia, but they are all very much smaller than the NT.

Where are the borders of the Northern Territory?

HOW MANY PEOPLE?

There are about 262,000 people in the Northern Territory. Most of the people in the Northern Territory live in or near Darwin.

Although the NT is the third largest state or territory of Australia, there are only two people per every ten square kilometres living there.

Indigenous Australians make up 26% of the Northern Territory's population. Compare this with the rest of Australia, where their numbers make up less than 4%.

(ABS 2021)

22% of people in the NT were not born in Australia. The main countries they came from are the Philippines, England and India.

ANCIENT LANDSCAPES

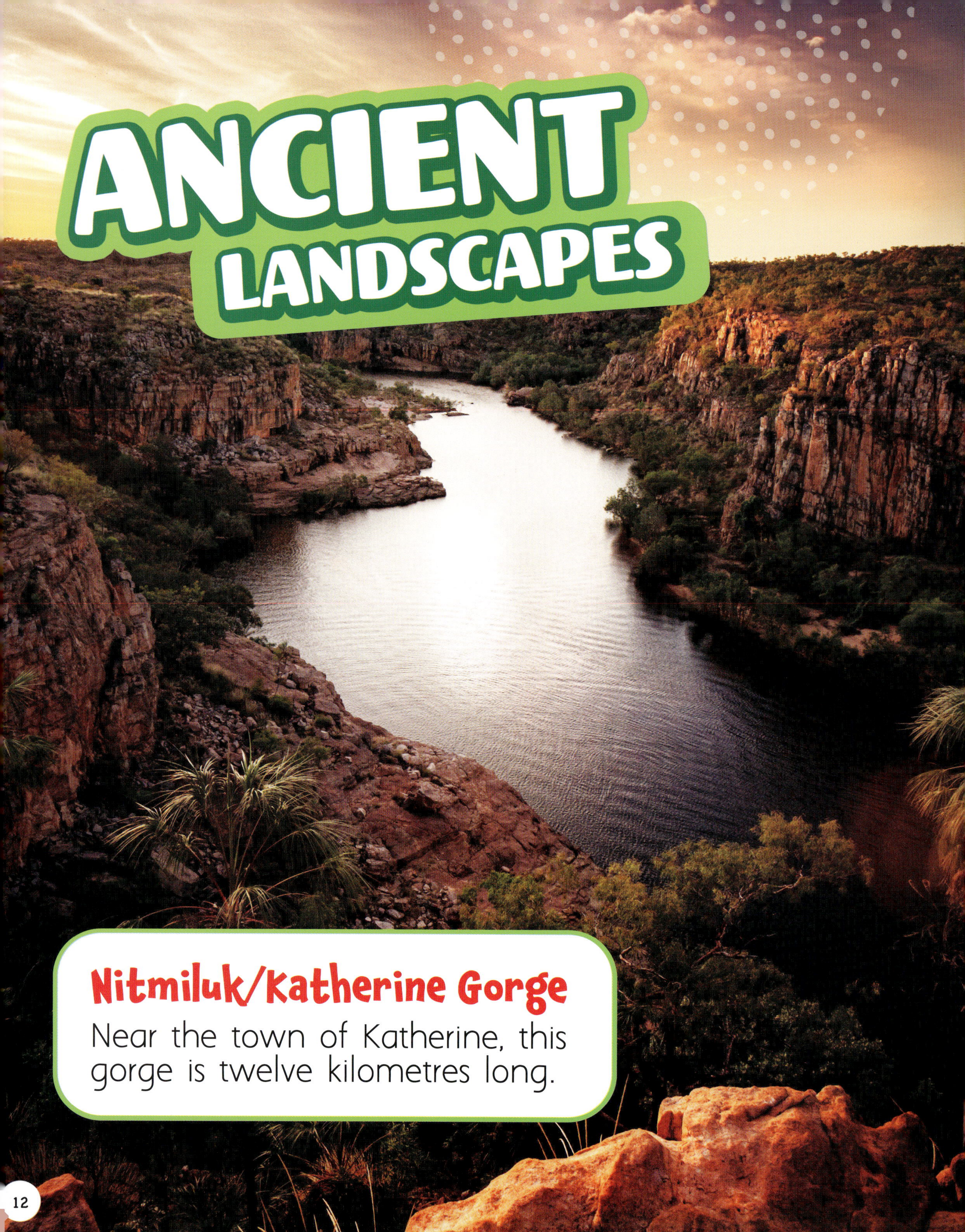

Nitmiluk/Katherine Gorge

Near the town of Katherine, this gorge is twelve kilometres long.

Karlu Karlu/Devils Marbles

These large boulders are scattered across a valley about 100 kilometres from Tennant Creek.

Kings Canyon

The canyon floor provides shelter from the heat for many plants and animals.

Kata Tjuta

A group of dome-shaped rocks about 50 kilometres from Uluru.

KAKADU

Kakadu is the largest national park in Australia. Some of the ancient rocks in the park date back to over 2,500 million years ago.

ULURU

Uluru is a giant sandstone rock in the desert. It is 300 metres high and goes down two kilometres underground. The town of Yulara, nearby, was built to look after the many tourists who visit Uluru.

THE BIGGEST CITIES

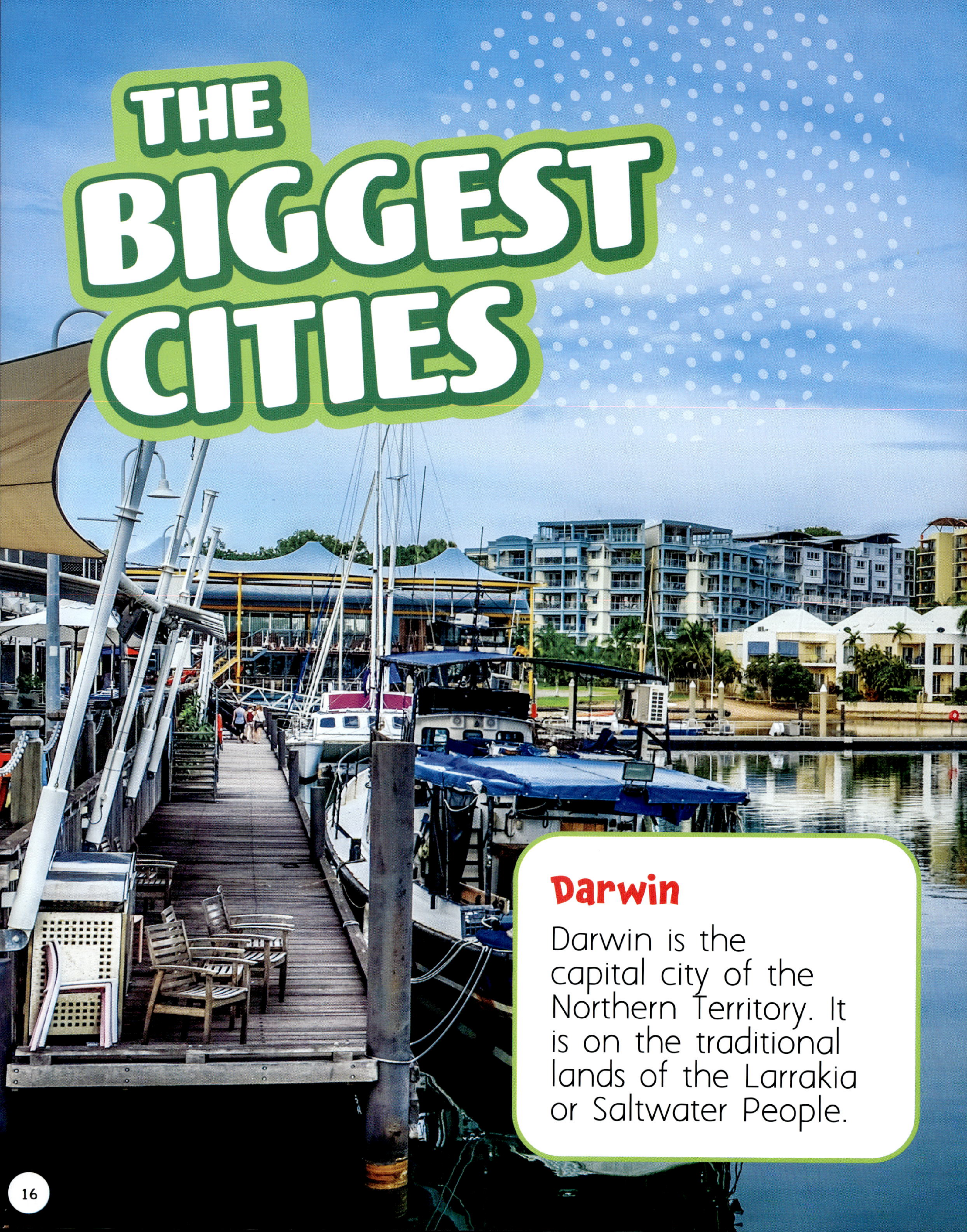

Darwin

Darwin is the capital city of the Northern Territory. It is on the traditional lands of the Larrakia or Saltwater People.

Alice Springs

Alice Springs is on Arrernte land. It is surrounded by deserts.

Palmerston

In 1869, a settlement called Palmerston was built at the place we now call Darwin.

Katherine

Although it is one of the biggest towns in the Northern Territory, Katherine's population is only about 10,000 people.

MINING AND BUSINESS

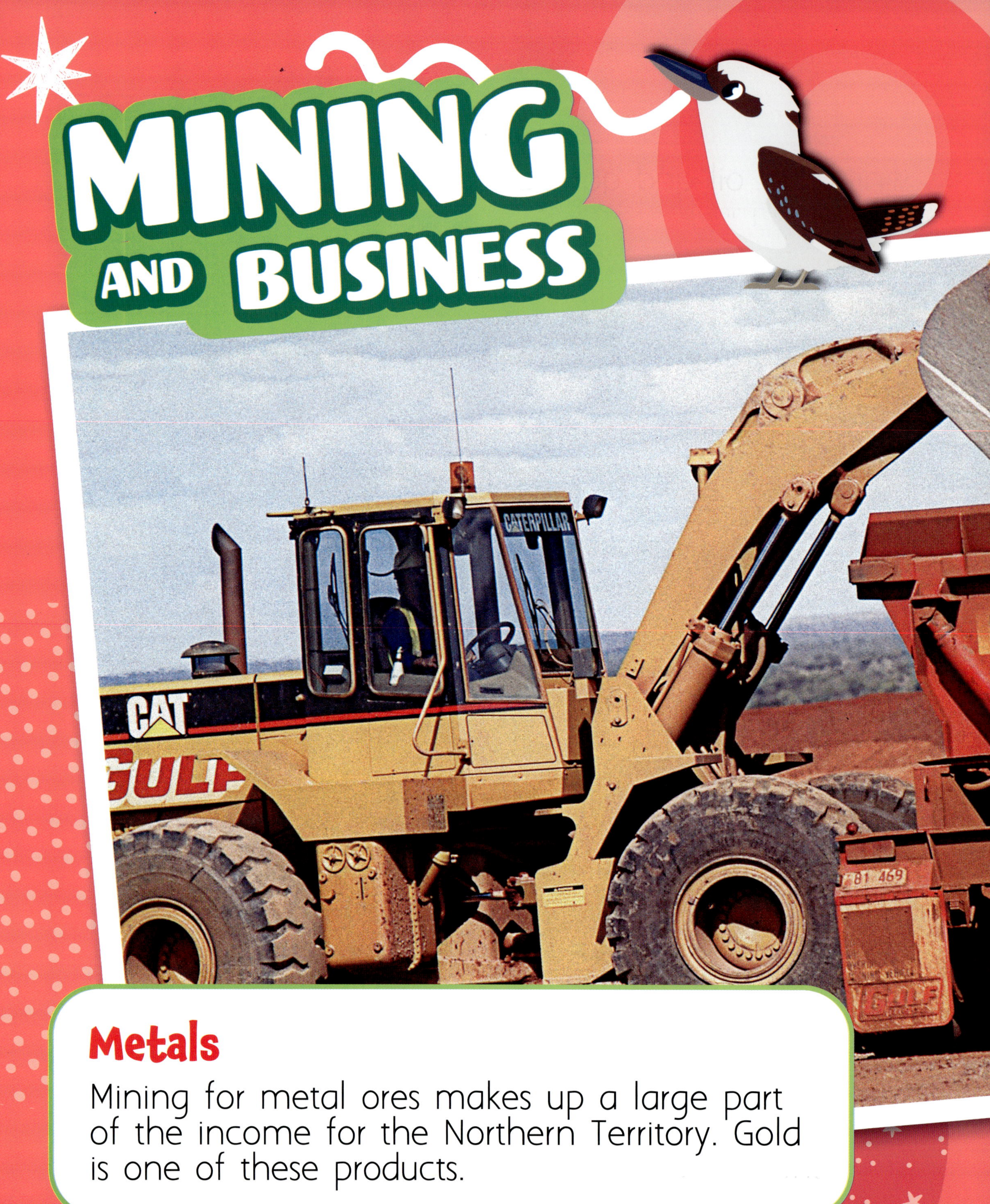

Metals

Mining for metal ores makes up a large part of the income for the Northern Territory. Gold is one of these products.

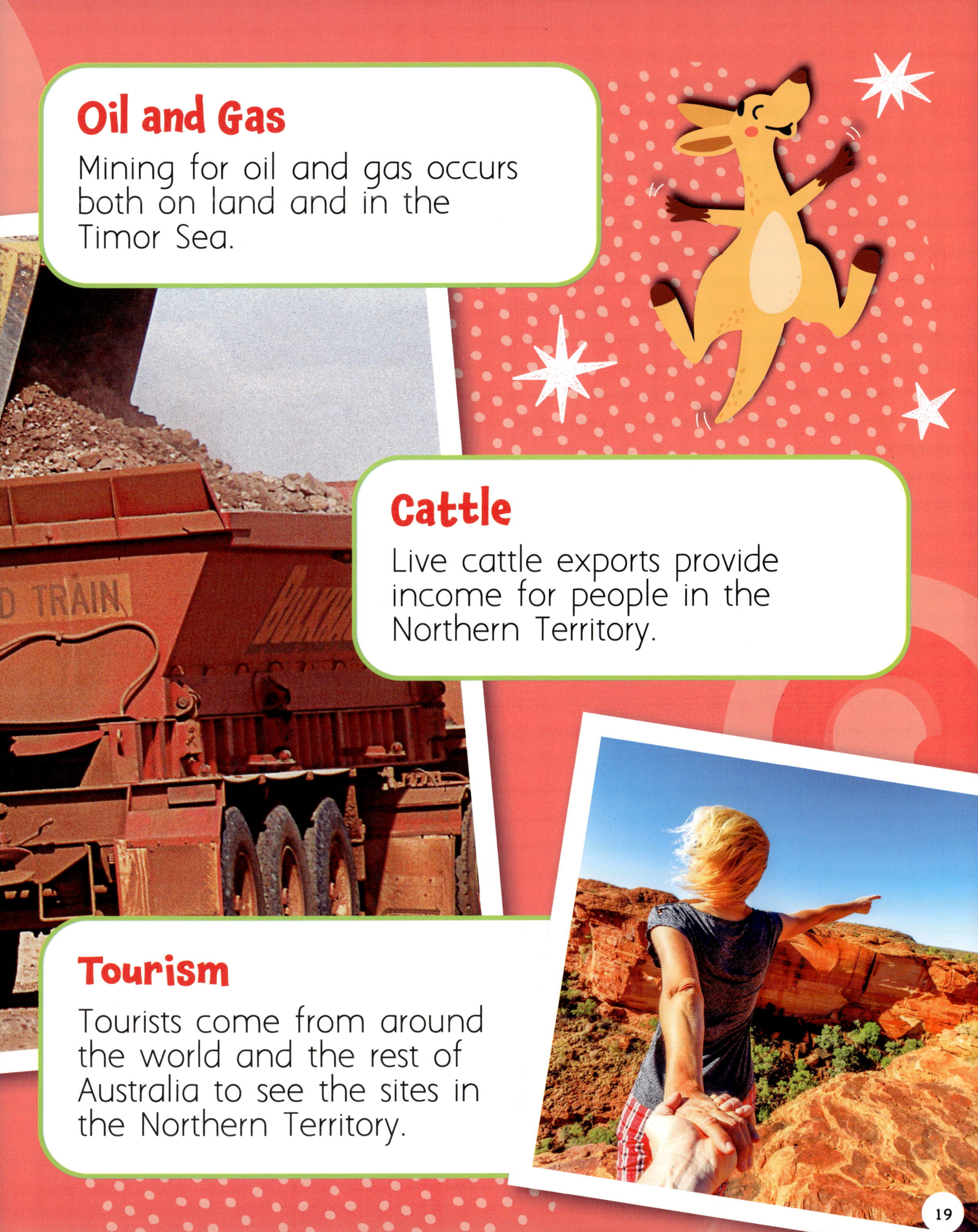

Oil and Gas

Mining for oil and gas occurs both on land and in the Timor Sea.

Cattle

Live cattle exports provide income for people in the Northern Territory.

Tourism

Tourists come from around the world and the rest of Australia to see the sites in the Northern Territory.

NORTHERN TERRITORY'S ISLANDS

Tiwi Islands

This island group includes Bathurst and Melville Islands. They are 100 kilometres north of Darwin and are home to the Tiwi people.

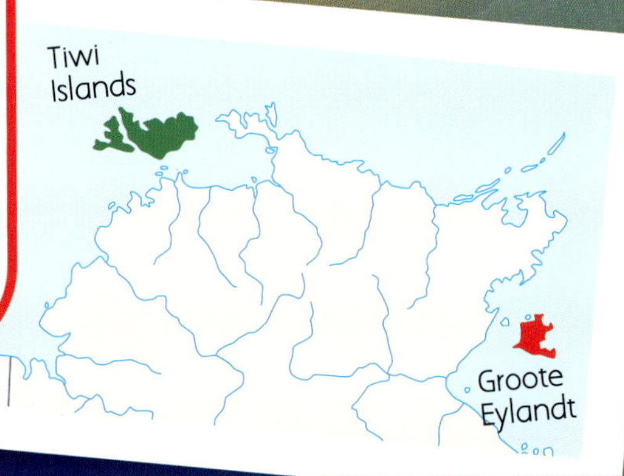

Groote Eylandt

The traditional owners of Groote Eylandt are the Anindilyakwa people. There are about forty smaller islands nearby, many of which are uninhabited.

NORTHERN TERRITORY'S DESERTS

Simpson Desert

Famous for its long sand dunes, the Simpson Desert is home to the endangered bilby. The camels in the desert come from the camels released after the Overland Telegraph Line was finished in 1872.

Tanami Desert

The Tanami Desert is one of the biggest in Australia. It covers more than one tenth of the Northern Territory.

GOVERNMENT OF THE NORTHERN TERRITORY

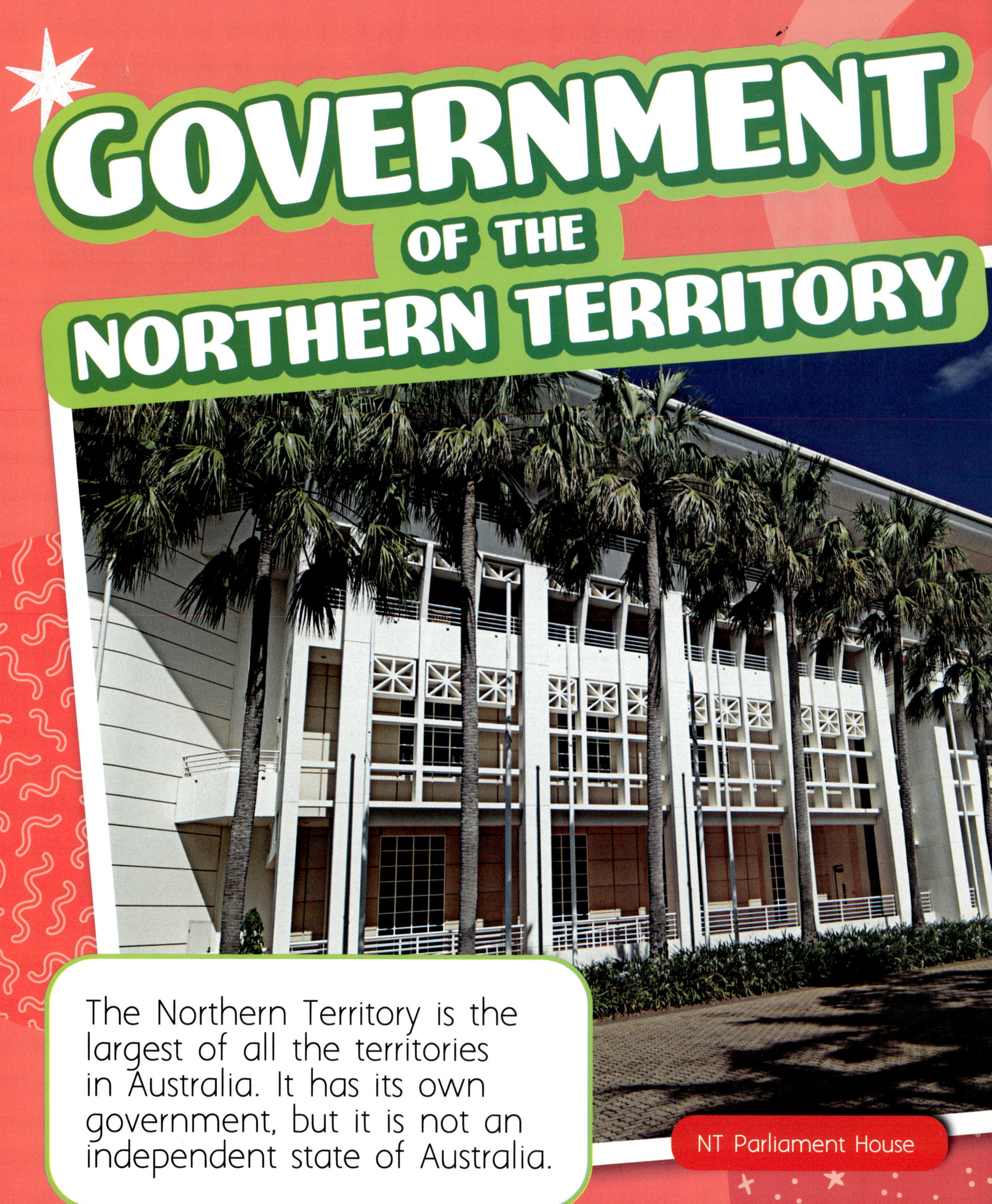

NT Parliament House

The Northern Territory is the largest of all the territories in Australia. It has its own government, but it is not an independent state of Australia.

Timeline

1788 - The NT was part of all the land claimed by the British when they arrived in NSW

1863 - The NT became part of SA

1869 - Settlers from Britain built Palmerston

1911 - The NT became a part of the new Commonwealth of Australia

1978 - The NT had its own government with just one House of Parliament

The new Parliament House in the NT was opened in 1994, after Cyclone Tracy destroyed the first building.

FLAGS OF THE NORTHERN TERRITORY

Australian Aboriginal Flag

The Aboriginal Flag was first flown in 1971. It was designed by elder Harold Thomas in 1970.

What the flag represents:

Yellow Disc	The Sun and yellow ochre
Red	The land
Black	The Aboriginal people of Australia

Flag of the NT

The NT flag dates from 1978. The five stars represent the Southern Cross stars, the flower is Sturt's desert rose, and the three colours of the NT flag are black, white and red ochre.

EMBLEMS OF THE NORTHERN TERRITORY

Floral Emblem
Sturt's desert rose

Animal Emblem
Red kangaroo

Bird Emblem
Wedge-tailed eagle

The Coat of Arms

This is a symbol of the Northern Territory and each part of it has a meaning:

Sturt's desert rose
The floral emblem of the NT

Red kangaroo
The animal emblem of the NT

Wedge-tailed eagle
The bird emblem of the NT

Shield
Decorated with Indigenous art

Kangaroos
Hold shells found along the coast

Eagle
Holds a Tjurunga stone

Helmet
Refers to the army

MONSOON

In the south of Australia, there are four seasons each year. In the NT, they have only two seasons.

Wet Season

The wet season is when there is a lot of rain and wind. This is the monsoon season and it starts in November.

Dry Season

In the dry season, which starts in May, there is not much rain, and the weather is very hot.

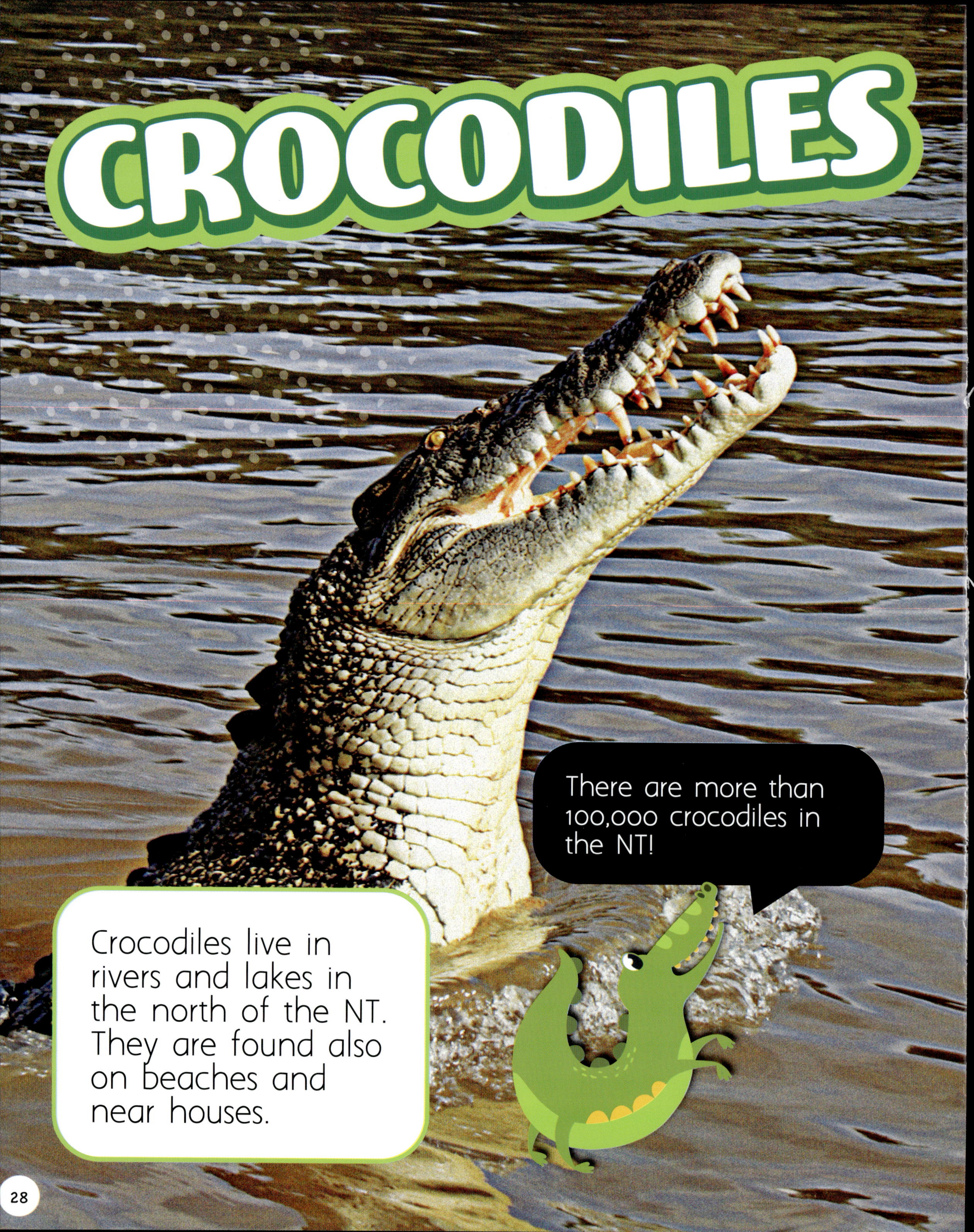
CROCODILES
There are more than
100,000 crocodiles in
the NT!
Crocodiles live in
rivers and lakes in
the north of the NT.
They are found also
on beaches and
near houses.

CYCLONE TRACY

Cyclone Tracy was Australia's worst cyclone in recent times. It happened in Darwin on Christmas Day, 1974. Most of the buildings in Darwin were blown down or damaged. Many people died.

THE GHAN

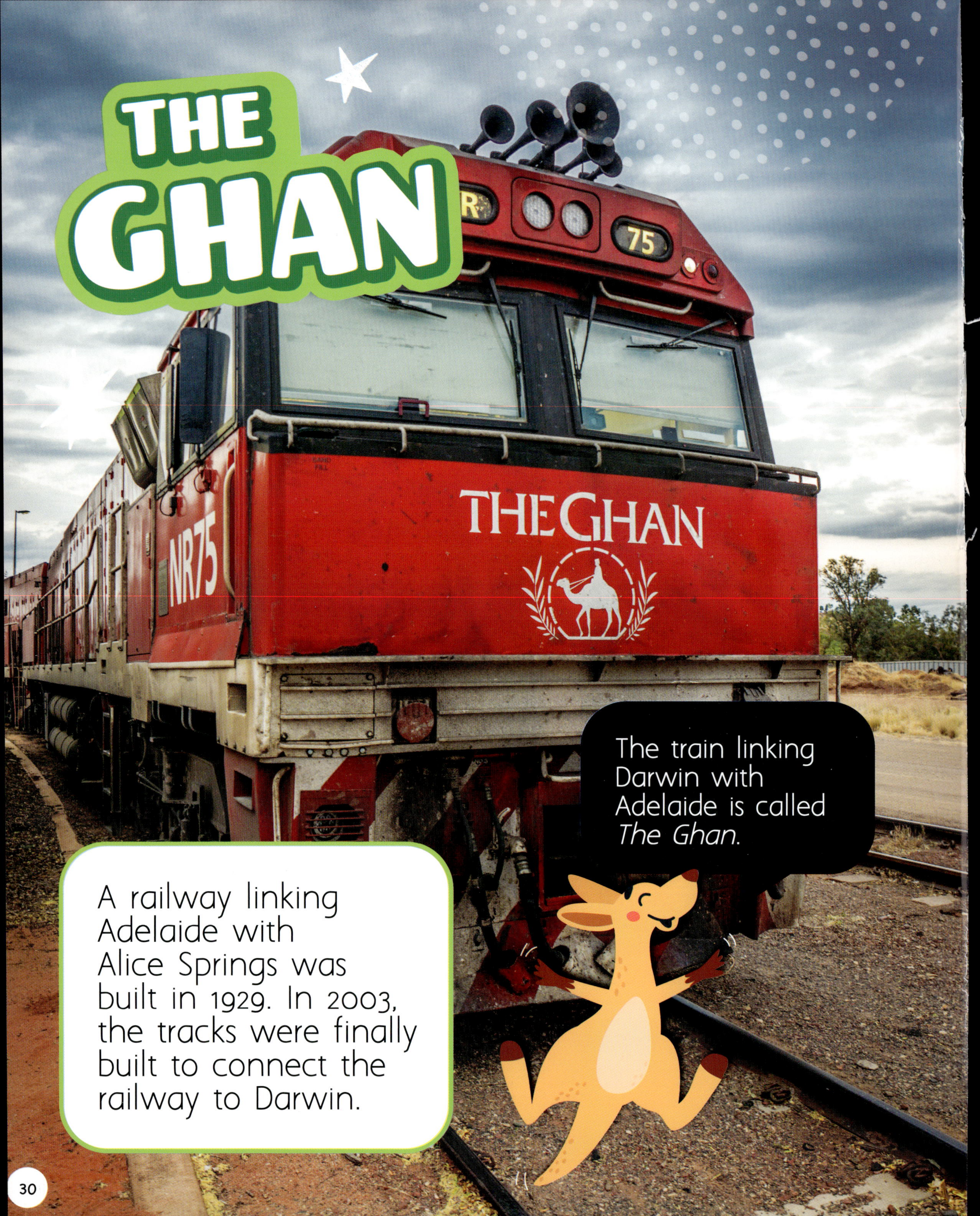

The train linking Darwin with Adelaide is called *The Ghan*.

A railway linking Adelaide with Alice Springs was built in 1929. In 2003, the tracks were finally built to connect the railway to Darwin.

GLOSSARY

boulder large, rounded rock

canyon deep valley

dome high rock with rounded top

dunes sand hills

emblem symbol

floral referring to flowers

gorge deep valley

mangrove tree that can grow in salty water

ochre crushed stone used for paint by Indigenous Australians

population number of people, or other living things

settlers people who move to live in a different country, usually as farmers

territory separate part of Australia that is not a state but is under the control of the Australian Government

traditional lands land that Indigenous Australians and their ancestors have lived on and used

uninhabited describes a place where nobody lives

Tanami Desert

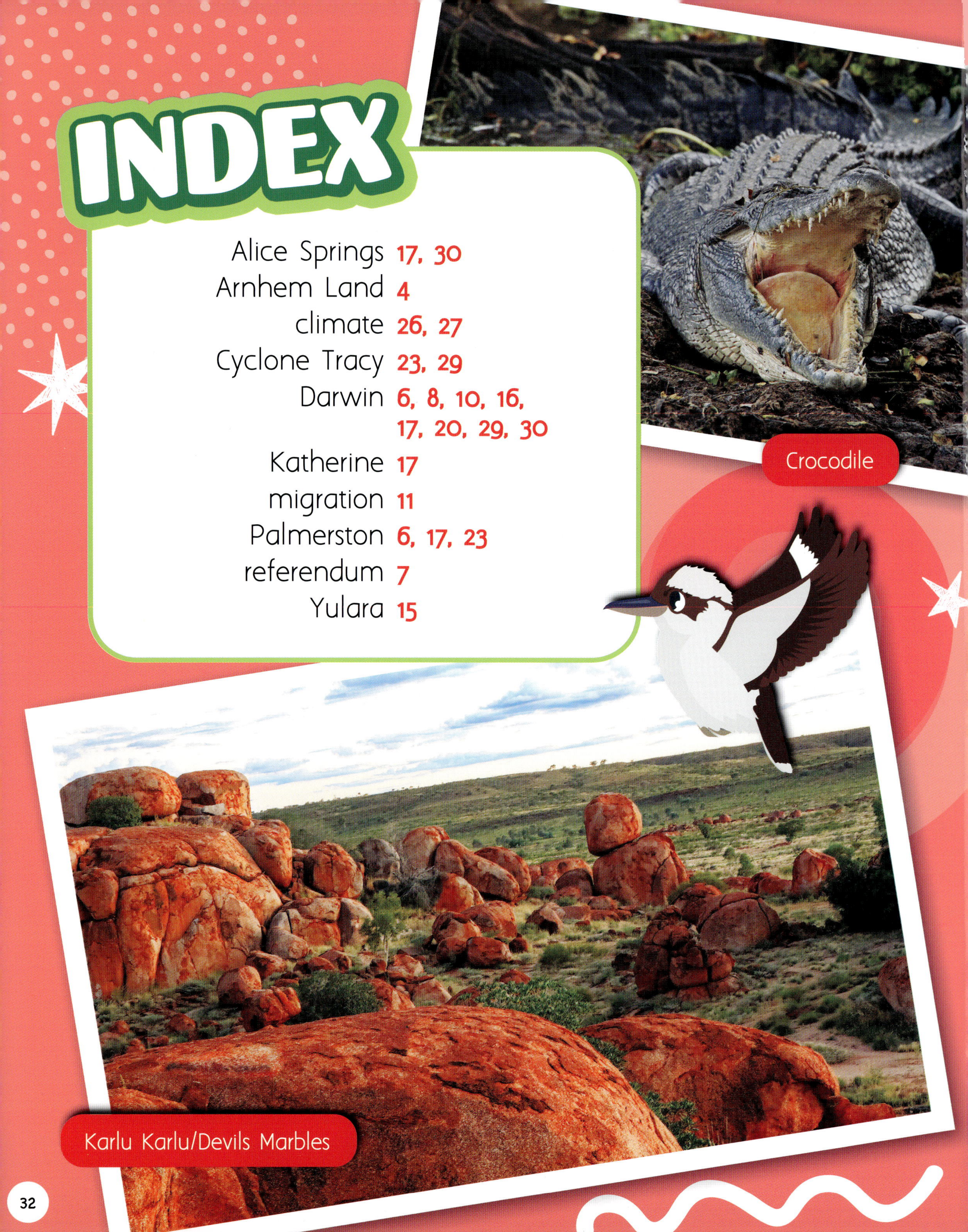

INDEX

Crocodile

Karlu Karlu/Devils Marbles

KIDS' GUIDE
TO
AUSTRALIA'S
STATES & TERRITORIES
NT
NORTHERN
TERRITORY
WA
WESTERN
AUSTRALIA